Time began in a garden.

Twenty Wild Decembers:
Poems on Time

by Jason Farley

Jason Farley *Twenty Wild Decembers: Poems on Time*
© 2018 by Jason Farley
All rights reserved.

Published by Jovial Press, 2106 E. 63rd, Spokane, WA 99223
www.jovial-pub.com
Printed in the United States of America

        17 18 19 20 21 22   9 8 7 6 5 4 3 2 1

ISBN: 0-9998050-1-0
ISBN-13: 978-0-9998050-1-5

The long slow slog
through publishing perils
can kill a man's dog
and make his cat feral.
But we persevere
in spite of the odds
like an old muleteer
with a wink and a plod.

FOREWORD

I am impatient. I listen to podcasts and audio books on double speed. I often skim when I read. I have too many speeding tickets (all but one well-deserved). I fit the manic panic of today's production-consumption culture. I know it is bad for me, but the pressure still does what pressure does. It presses.

Poetry slows me. Whether the thumping rhythms of the ancients or the jazzed out cadences of contemporary poets, poetry takes time. To read poetry you must decelerate. Poetry pumps the brakes. It has been a source of rest and provided space for breath to settle into a rhythm. Time to wrestle with my thoughts, with my life, and with my God. And even though I often come away limping, I come away blessed.

We often misread the unhurried as lazy. Even when I am the unhurried. We feel guilt in ease. But God commands us to rest and, like every command of God, He is loving us by commanding us to imitate him. Being that he is the most alive—the most vibrantly buoyant—of all beings, his commands are a call to be more fully alive.

This collection represents my attempts to continue slowing myself to write poems. If it helps you to slow yourself to read and rest, I will be content. These poems swirl around the theme of time. Time passing. Time having passed. I do hope that you will find them worth your time.

Jason Farley
Jovial Hall, Spokane
Hay Moon, 2018 AD

CONTENTS

Preface	v
Foreword	vii
Dedication	
Sunday	3
Monday	17
Tuesday	23
Wednesday	31
Thursday	39
Friday	45
Saturday	53
Glossary	61

DEDICATION
To My Wife as We Begin Our 18th Year

An inmate of your mineral,
you ensorcel my soul.
Drop copper in my bowl
of quicksilver. I am ephemeral.
You are the sea. I am littoral.
You are the temple. I am dipteral.
You are the poem. I am doggerel.
You are the sun. I the cockerel.

Wednesday is gripped and warmed
entering Friday's vital center.
Smell of manuscript ink, the tempter's
zinc, always laughs and storms.
You are the shape. I am the form.
You are life's force. I am reborn.
You little boy blue. I the horn.
You are the dawn. I am the morn.

Twenty Wild Decembers:
Poems on Time

Twenty Wild Decembers

Poems on Time

Sunday

Twenty Wild Decembers

Poems on Time

TWENTY WILD DECEMBERS

Twenty wild Decembers all have melted into spring.
Twenty snowmelts guggled down these shaded tree-tipped valley streams.
Twenty summers. Twenty! Twenty summers in a blink.

The rocks, they have not noticed, nor do give a susurration,
that full twenty times the sun has coursed a tint on the horizon.
Yet here the trees can hear the breeze breathe, 'Chronos is a Titan.'

Twenty summers. Twenty! Twenty summers Saturn's cloven.
Time has woven golden poems, twenty times it does embolden,
or at least has broken open courage, molten in its motion.

For I am old now, I am old, my trousers rolled up at the bottom.
Twenty years kept passing since her death came dark and ill-begotten.
And the pain, the deep leaf-mold, seeding roots I've not forgotten

That then raised a gnarly tree of toughly merciful compassion
shading all the scarred and scared, and fruiting heaven's heavy ration.
These lation's lasting pains, I know, are how I've been refashioned.
For earth's draftsman/artist/mason can be trusted with my passion.

Twenty Wild Decembers

PETRICHOR

Petrichor (noun): A pleasant smell that frequently accompanies the first rain after a long period of warm, dry weather (OED).

There's a word for that.
Petrichor. A word to differentiate
the smell of the first rain
after a drought. But I wonder,

is it truly its own smell?
Is it not, perhaps,
just that our noses
become accustomed
to the regular smell
of a regular day.
It could be that
we simply cease to notice
regular goodnesses,
habitual beauty,
everyday glory,
without the particles of dry dust
invading our cilia.
It could be that we become
comfortably noseblind
without drought.

Perhaps all smells are petrichor,
but our nose can only
be trained to recognize it
by thirst.

Dry spell may just be
the necessary precondition
of true-tuned scent recognition.
An arid stretch might be the way
to reset the vibrissae.
Then they will again stand at attention.
Catch again the petrichor that,

Poems on Time

—through familiarity—
has been slipping past the watch
unnoticed.
Unenjoyed.

Twenty Wild Decembers

A LONG ENGAGEMENT

After a long winter
the sun comes again.
Sometimes at least. And today?
Today was one of those sometimes.

But when mid-winter-spring sun comes
it fails to heat. At least
not at first. At first sunlight
sings only the promise of heat.

And though sometimes it seems
like a faithless tease,
it always, eventually, delivers.
At least here. With me.

But the wait, at least
sometimes—to me, mind you—
seems like a long engagement.
Impatient for oneness.

Waiting for hoping
to become being.
For faith
to become sight.

Poems on Time

FULLNESS OF TIMES

Mary was in labor.
The times were full.
And she was great
with Child,

On countless occasions
throughout our world's history
this story's been told.
Babies are born in all times,
in all sorts of places.
Yet this had never happened before.
Virgins don't have
babies. Joseph and young Mary knew
what made babies.
This was inconceivable. Except
with God, all things are possible.

Time began in a garden,
with a dragon, a tree, some lust
of the flesh, lust
of the eyes, the pride
of life. That was an empty time.
A naked time.
A hungry time.
But God,
God started to fill.
The weak and beggarly elements had us then.
Time was empty;
we were hungry.
Sold our inheritance
for a bite. But God
sacrificed in our place
an animal. Gave us fur coats
and promises.
Promises of more to come.
Time was still empty.

Twenty Wild Decembers

We were still hungry,
but warm.

Sin, God warned, crouched at our door.
Anyone who hates his brother in his heart
is a murderer. Like the dragon;
a murderer, a liar, from the beginning.
Cain filled his ears with wax.
Lashed his soul to the mast
and held back from beauty.
Thought that he was hungry because his brother was full.
Still happens all of the time.
Empty times sometimes lead to hungry souls.
Sometimes empty souls,
looking for a fill,
empty the world.
And we did,

Until only eight souls were saved through water.
God undid what our hungry souls had wrought
munching on lotus
and one another.
But God began to fill
the time, and we eight, we ate with God.
Seven of every clean animal
to make a feast to God in that New Earth.
After the dove hovered
over the face
of gathered waters,
the dry land reappeared.

But that was only the beginning of the filling.
The times were mostly still empty.
Still under the elements,
God called Father Abraham out of Ur.
"Go" he said. We went.
A rich young ruler
selling all we had in Ur.

Poems on Time

Richer with nothing
plus the promise.
"The times will be full someday.
A seed will come someday.
The world will be full, someday,
of people with faith like yours,
Abraham. Someday.
Now the whole world is hungry,
but she will not always be."

And the famine ending banquet
will be born through Isaac.
Dawn's rose red fingers are feast-full
Satiation's on the horizon.
"So take him up the mountain.
Show me that you believe
in the resurrection."
A thicket-crowned ram
concealing a full-time.

There were still times to fill.
God gave us Joseph to lead us,
but we sold our inheritance
for a bowl of hungry freedom.
God intended to feed us
through Joseph, and our puny mutinies
never kept God from filling us
when he said he would.
Another time filled
with us landing in Goshen
– like Eden's Garden.
But our belly was our god,
preferring slavery with cucumbers,
grown slow in a garden,
to freedom with morning-thrown manna.
under angel tables.
Even dogs eat crumbs.

Twenty Wild Decembers

God filled our wilderness-stomachs,
but the times were still empty.
We marched around Jericho, choir out front.
The walls fall
when the call to worship is blown.
Sin crouched and we were conquered,
God sent us Judges to save us.
We asked for a King and picked
 the failure who cowered in Goliath's shadow.
God anointed us a giant-killer.
A Hermes with five smooth stones.
A petrapentateuch.
Only needed one.
Goliath's own sword dripping. Peace,
Peace, for the whole land.
Another time full.

But God's house was still a tent.
He wanted us to pitch a permanent place.
He wanted David's son to build it.
The temple went up.
We were so close now.
Gold Garden,
fruitful land,
but Solomon's wisdom
failed to hold.
Other gods offered
to tell us their secrets.
They lied of course.
Public truth is common.
but secret meat is sweet.

We forgot then.
We watched the temple disintegrate.
We stopped tabling with God,
returned the feast-invitations.
But God hunted the highways
and bird-dogged the byways

Poems on Time

to find us a child king.
Another time full.

King Josiah, contractor for God's house,
prepared a place for us
to eat with Him again.
The child-king had faith
To see why we were hungry.
He knew what would finally fill us,
The law was found in the temple walls.
Sin revived.
We went after the other nation's gods.
Told them our God had left
on a business trip.
Invited them into our beds and our boards.
God knocked down the temple and sent us away.
Another time full.
But now, exile.
We wanted their gods.
We got them.
Hungry times

God spoke
with Nebuchanezzer. Sometimes
he listened, sometimes
he didn't. He was fickle.
Right leader for a fickle people.
When God told him
his gold empire was temporary
only the head and not the whole,
he tried to resist the truth.
Midas-ed his future in statue.
Tossed to and fro,
God shut the mouth of lions for him.
Cooled furnace flames for him,
and eventually, after a time
with the donkeys, he cracked.
God's grace ran him down.

Twenty Wild Decembers

God's grace not leaving us to ourselves.
God's white tiger-jawed grace
catching our gazelle-legged rebellion.
But the time was only beginning to fill.

God called Cyrus before he was born
to be his King of kings
and fill the times.
The seductive curves of wisdom
Crying from his right hand.
Esther filling queen's throne
and such a time as this.

We remembered then.
There had been a time
when we lived in our own land.
And God had been a good
neighbor. When he had found us
Thug-beat on the side of the road.
He had set us up at hotel Babylon.
Paid for everything.
Hadn't he mentioned
that he would come back
and pay his tab in 70 years?
and check on us in 70 years?
and give us rest in 70 years?
We learned later
that he had come with us.
So distracted, feeding pigs in our hunger
wondering what our father's house-servants
had for dinner,
we passed over the God-with-us.

But then the news came.
Go home. God told Cyrus,
that this time was full.
We went and got Ezra.
(A library-rat is easy to find).

Poems on Time

And then Nehemiah
and Mordecai. It took a while,
but we put the temple back up.
It looked smaller.
Some of the old wept.
Ezekiel cried,
"See by faith, not sight.
This rebuilt temple is towering.
God himself will walk
past these cherubim,
through these doors.
into this garden
in the cool of the morning."
Another time full.
Clean water. Heart tablets
exchanged for stone.

"Keep an eye on Bethlehem.
Look for Elijah.
Expect a little virgin-born child."
The times stretch
reaching to be full.
Promises pitch near fulfillment.
Heavens itch
to be rolled up like a scroll.
Stars hitch in excitement
frequenting choir practices.
The Spheres practicing their accompaniments.

And now the times
were full. God
was making his move.
The King of kings gestating royally.
The Lord joying
to break heavy yokes.
To set the captives free.
The blind will see.
The deaf will hear.

Twenty Wild Decembers

The lame will get up and dance
because the governments will all be
on these little shoulders,
born of a woman,
born under the law.
The fullness of times had come.
The dragon-slayer was here,
light yokes in his wake,
Sun, Moon, Mercury, Venus
Mars, Jupiter, Saturn
all in his right hand.
Hard-heel for the serpent's head.
Set to toss
the weak and beggarly elements.
Fear banished.
Guilt broken.
Shame skewered
and death dispatched.
The Son of the Father was here.
We will all now,
in this time, be sons.

Mary was in labor.
No room for her in the inn.
The child was coming
to bring us out of exile.
Being born in Exile would work.
It even made sense.
Hungry all of this time.
Thirsty all of this time.
For the bread of life.
For living water.
And now . . .
now the times
were full.
It was time.
Time for
Emmanuel.

Poems on Time

Monday

Twenty Wild Decembers

Poems on Time

SONG OF YOUR OWN

People take on the shape of the songs and stories that surround them, especially if they don't have a song of their own. Neil Gaiman, Anansi Boys

Like the slender-ankled daughters of ocean
shaped by the banks that decide their path,
we are shaped by our songs and our stories like potions.
Each dent-cut puddle is an idiopath.

Giving us guise like a whittlers tools.
The stories and songs that we're told and we're sung,
the dances we dance are how the soul's school
retunes the heart-lute *real life* has unstrung.

So attend to the music, behear to the song.
Long to ascend to the *what* you were made for.
Raid the brigade of old lore to belong
to the Milky Way's hymn of the rising lodestar.

Twenty Wild Decembers

NO LONE-ISLE DOWN IN THE CITY

I will arise and go now, down to my flat in the valley.
To my small apartment there on the seventeenth floor.
With windows facing East there, overlooking my city,
And live with the million I'm made for.

And I shall hunt for peace there, for peace rising floor by floor.
Rising as the coffee brews to where the street lights glow.
There midnight's neon lifts us together as we forget our color.
And table-life taste our tomorrow.

I will arise and go now, for always day and night
I hear the Deep's laugh as we love one-another
While I walk in a crowd soul caught like a kite
I hear my heart beat in my brother.

Poems on Time

THERE ARE NO SAD WORDS

There are no sad words in the dictionary.
They only fill with sorrow when slipped
or stormed into story, or rhyme.

Hamlet might become a blissful burg,
full of smiles stretched on children's faces,
caroling cheeks shining as they dance in the falling snow.

Or Hamlet pivots inward.
Is surviving worth the existential torment?
Shall Hamlet, when so sad, even be?

But in the dictionary, *hamlet* is not heartsick.
Only snug and unfeeling. Resting and reposed.
Even death is not sad, wedged between deasil and debacle.

It waits to be storied into essence as
some shaking child's salvation.
When the monster in the closet meets the death in daddy's hand.

Or death may lose its sting,
in the grip of one more mirthful than the grave-
clothes, than the rolled-stone, than the clay could ever hold.

There are no sad words in the dictionary.
Only half-told tales and partial rhymes
All waiting on the punch line.

CLOUDS WILL PASS

The stars all wait
in vestral hope
to dance their cosmic rite

while clouds cut
shards of the sunlight seam
into arrows of piercing bright.

Hit with a shaft of light
that bursts as it pierces
my living middle,

God's eye diffuses a quickening
ray and the shadows
shine like nickel.

Clouds will pass in every sky.
Shadows crawl the country.
The tiptoed steps that brought me through
turned out to be God's pedantry.

Poems on Time

Tuesday

Twenty Wild Decembers

Poems on Time

TRUTH'S CONSTANT

Truth always comes with constant combat.
Ever-watching, every night
it lays its head with blackened eyes,
nose crunched, crooked from the fight.

But truth, it fights for other's freedom.
Fights to set the prisoner free.
Truth, in love, breaks our shackles,
cuts down slavery and Thor's Oak Tree.

Twenty Wild Decembers

THE HEEL-STONE

And the LORD God said unto the serpent, Because thou hast done this, thou art cursed above all cattle, and above every beast of the field; upon thy belly shalt thou go, and dust shalt thou eat all the days of thy life: And I will put enmity between thee and the woman, and between thy seed and her seed; it shall bruise thy head, and thou shalt bruise his heel. Genesis 3:14-15

Wars and seed and bruises.
Our God promised us
wars and seed and bruises.
But we would win
in the end.
The dragon's curse—our promise—
is a man with a heel.
A seed with a heel.
A dragon skull crushed.

Cain? Is this the man?
The Lord gave him.
But the first shall be last
and the last first. Sin crouched.
The murderer from the beginning,
like a lion prowling
for devourable
whispering for blood.
"Raca," roared Cain.
The dust caught the blood.
The mud cried for blood.

The first new heart, won by the wandering lion
learned jealousy. Hate.
And the ground cried for justice.
And the ground began to recall.
The seed's blood watered thorns
and thistles. The waters covered
the earth again,
but the rinsed acres remembered.

Poems on Time

God called our father out of Ur
with a seed-promise. Remember!
"A seed is coming. A strong heel is coming.
With nation-blessings.
Show me that you believe, Abraham.
The dragon's head will be
short-lived, Abraham.
Rise up early.
Lead Isaac up the mountain, Abraham.
I will provide a seed.
Do not withhold yours, Abraham.
Abraham, do you believe I
    raise the dead?'

We were Abraham's seed,
but without his seed-faith.
We forgot resurrection
and regarded to other gods.
Egyptian gods whispered sweetly
over the cucumbers,
"Hath God said a seed?"
Munched a route back into slavery.
But God remembered.
God had said Seed.
His ten toes flexed
to crush the ten gods of Egypt.
Finished with the first born.
Heel on the seed of the Egyptians.
Sheltered our seed, safe in the wilderness.
Watered the dry land as we passed.

The serpent mistook the signs.
Never resigned.
He tried giants.
Played right into God's hand.

Twenty Wild Decembers

Strength is never shown in strength.
Og and Bashan echoed when they fell.
Faith bred in Babylon still heard the stomp.

"Do not forget" God said.
Piled enemies at our gates.
Enemies with hairy heads.
Each dome a memorial.
Jael, wife of Heber, welcomed Cicera.
Abimalech had no faith. Never looked up.
Heads crushed at God's new beginning.

Tall Saul was faith-short.
Blind leading the blind.
Too blind too see Goliath's
shaggy forehead. David saw
seed, five smooth stones, and a promise.
More than enough.
Brought the head back
dripping with sermon.
"God forgives sins.
God keeps his promises.
God Emmanuel"

The bushy scalp of the dragon's house.
Wound upon wound.
War and seed and bruises.
But God delivered a home as promised.
The dragon still roared,
and ruled, and wrecked in the wilderness.
But God settled us.
Multiplied us.
Moved in with us.
Filled us with laws
and wisdom and music
that made the serpent's seed jealous.
"Who has a God so close?"
"Who has laws so just?"

Poems on Time

"Who has a king so wise?"
"Sing us one of the songs of Zion."
We sang.
We sang the promise.
We sang the heel-stone.
We sang the seed-war.
Blessed is he. The one coming.
The head crusher
for the serpent's seed.

The stone, bruised
to water the flocks and herds and church.
The stone pounded
into a nail for the tent of Jael.
The stone that jangled in a shepherd's pouch
with four others stream-smoothed.
The stone that ground grain
and the head of Abimalech.
The stone that caught
Jezebel's skull as she fell.
The stone carved without hands,
to break clay-iron toes.
The stone grown
to cover the globe.
The stone that stumbled the blind leading the blind.

The stone rejected and refused. Hurled by Polyphemus.
Receiver of three nail stones, a serpent lifted up.
The stone sent for the corner of a living temple
breathed his last
to build with breathing stones.
The heel-stone.
The heart-stone,
crushing to dust.
A stone of stumbling,
A rock of offense.
The heel-stone.

Twenty Wild Decembers

Son of Adam, son of Abraham, son of David.
Seed of Adam, seed of Abraham, seed of David.
This, the man,
wet with anointing. Whet for battle.
Hell in train—legion of winged things
held back on easeful wings—
heel itching to flatten wyrm-skull.
Strong man bound. Lying tongue tied.
Time to empty the house.
Time to sweep it clean.

Healing? Moses did that.
Cleanse the leper? Raise the dead? Elisha did that.
But commanding devils?
Even Michael the Archangel only said, "The Lord rebuke you."
They covered eyes.
They held mouths.
They struck us with lunacy
until we writhed, and foamed.
They stopped ears.
They threw us into the fire
and into the water.
But then
the Word.
The Word spoken when the morning stars sang together;
the Word dwelt
and the Word spoke,
And the spirits slumped prostrate.
The spirits said, "Son of God."
A house promised to fall divides.
Wars and seeds and bruises.

We were thirsty,
the Water became wine.
We were hungry
The Stone became bread
It was time to unfence the table.

Poems on Time

"This is my body broken for you. Take and Eat."
Judas took. Judas Ate. And the Devil entered into him.
Some of you have fallen asleep.
Others have become possessed.
Faithless eating. Too dangerous.

We passed through the waters
into a new name.
Tongues of fire melted us.
Melded us to the growing;
to the groaning right-hand stone.
Our sewn lips were cut

As Moses lifted up the dragon
in the wilderness, so must the Son of Man be.
Yeshua Ha'Netzeret V'mlech Ha'Yehudim
They stripped off his clothes.
—There were principalities to strip—
Ἰησοῦς ὁ Ναζωραῖος ὁ βασιλεὺς τῶν Ἰουδαίων
His hands and feet were nailed.
—There were powers to conquer—
Iesus Nazarenus, Rex Iudaeorum
Eli, Eli, lama sabachthani?
He cried again with a loud voice
and gave up the ghost.
—There were crowns to capture—
Jesus of Nazareth, King of the Jews

The ground remembered all of the blood from Able.
The ground remembered all of the blood to Zechariah.
The ground knew the dead's taste.
The ground swallowed up our dragon-slayer.
Life's an unfamiliar flavor.
The Son of God was manifested,
to destroy the devil's works.
Took on mortal flesh:
That, through death, he might destroy
him that had death's power.

Twenty Wild Decembers

That death might swallow Death.
Dragon skulls echo when they crack.
Wars and seed and bruises.
The God of peace went to war.
Children of the Gd of Peace
now playing at the asp den.
The God of peace may soon crush Satan.
May soon crush Satan
underneath your feet.

Poems on Time

Wednesday

Twenty Wild Decembers

Poems on Time

DEAD MAN WALKING
Romans 6

Dead man walking
stalking like a lion.
Stylus poised. Pencil paused.

Flawed eyes and ears.
Years of fears flowering
into towering life-crash.

A rash death-swallowing,
following the cursed one.
Burst sun buried.

Hurried across the sky
and cross-stitched
—bewitched— below spiderweb-gravestone.

Brave alone, alone, (never) alone.

Twenty Wild Decembers

BREAD-BREAKING

Hospitality, that by-product of praise,
is awe in practice. Eden lost being
found. Low-hanging breadfruit, heavy on the branch,
as life-love becomes an everywhere hum.
A thrum that, like water in a mountain stream,
joys in the downward dance of a bouncing spring.

Poems on Time

PRODIGAL AT THE END OF THE TETHER

Like a wandering donkey that is swaggering and thundering,
he lumbered out from under-wing to quarter as an underling.

Doddering and tottering he shuttered until suffering
had water-whelmed the offering with gutterfuls of gristled weeping.

Heaven-fallen fire alone could scatter sodden epithets.
No idol-light or cheery slight, could smile away the dripping wet.

This drinking, spinning, pining, whining grizzle-irrigated soul
needs more than some clichéd riposte, echoed from an echo's loam.

He requires an appetite earthquake.
A shuffling of his deepest loves
A jackboot of bitterroot
pushing on his skinny neck,
pushing him to resurrect.

Twenty Wild Decembers

Poems on Time

Thursday

Twenty Wild Decembers

Poems on Time

100 PROOF BLUES

Resting his forehead deep in his hands,
sunburned, salted with the shadowland's sands.
He breathed in deep, and sighed from the sole
of his socks to the lair of his monopole soul.

Shoulders slumped under the weight of Gibraltar.
Tongue limp and dry as a smoldering Psalter.
Sepulcure ribcage-crankcaseing a sump pump
draining a mulish old stump of a swamp.

He said, "I have always been true to my heart.
True to the ocean, and true to my art.
True to myself, I sought every pleasure
I always had only myself as the measure.

And so I have always attained to the standard
For I was the benchmark, the baseline, the canon.
Never had minions, only married the ocean.
The surf was my mistress, my only devotion.

And now I'm alone. I am old and worn down.
Icebound at sundown. All alone in midtown.
Lame fettered limbs limply groan on this throne.
My heart of sharp stone has grown cold alone.

This world still survives by crook and by tooth.
And this world, it still loves me by bruise and by noose.
Crawling and crashing like a kelp-clogged wave,
beach-born and sprawling, caravaning her slaves.

I have seen beauty and stopped, out of words,
before women, and waves, and sunset firebirds.
But did I give myself to the beauty I saw?
I held back, bulwarked against bonds of awe.

Twenty Wild Decembers

I once rode the wave that everyone wanted.
Dropped in and held, fanatically dogged.
In search of the wave that would make it all worth it.
Monomaniacally phantasmagoric.

My eyes that once burned with dark red fire,
and churned in the surf of a yearning desire,
are now orange-embered coals. The starfire has smoldered.
Unremembered splendor surrendered for cold earth.

100 proof blues, so true they fooled
me out of my youth and my last pair of boots.
A rising tide, a clouding shroud,
solitary confinement in the middle of a crowd.

The rolling hint of mermaids, singing each to each.
Swelling, crashing Majesty that puts Himself in reach,
has filled to the brim these low hanging ears.
As forgotten as a sightseers cheap souvenirs,
I now hear the crash of the surf-wasted years."

Poems on Time

COLD BREEZE

Cold breeze, artfully inching up my pant leg
subtly sneaking through my socks
and stealing the spirit and warmth
of my toes and ankles.

The draft is not honest.
The breeze is not frank.
It does not straightforwardly warn you
that it is stealing your fire.

It sets an ambush
Calculating. Foxy. Wily.
The wind worms up and in
where no one else could go.

Other times it comes
blasting at coastlines,
playing pickup sticks
with full grown trees.

There is no stopping the wind
when the gusts and blasts
that squall and blow
are set on our destruction.

It blows where it wants. A prophet,
camel-haired, with locust legs
in her teeth, forest fire eyes,
and dark drafts for hair.

Twenty Wild Decembers

BUTTERMILK PANCAKES
For Cedric at Graduation

To get the very best pancakes
only buttermilk will do.
For proper buttermilk,
cream must be abused.
There is no glory
but resurrection glory.
No true story that is not death-gory.
The cream was bruised,
broken. Butter stolen.
Sour-sauce tossed off.
Striken, smitten, and afflicted,
shaken through great tribulation.

Only then, less-butter, less-glory,
Can it grapple with baking powder.
"You are my cake batter,
this day I have begotten thee."
Declared to be mine with the power
of an extra-wide spatula
Mickey Mouse ears,
chocolate chips
and frozen blackberries.

Poems on Time

Friday

Twenty Wild Decembers

Poems on Time

NOT EVERY APPLE, BUT THIS PARTICULAR ONE
"Life is a noun. Like bird." — Ben Palpant

I would like to write poetry consistently.
Like it was a job.
As if there would be consequences if I were late.
Like I would be fired if I didn't show up
    and see.
I would, then, be required to stop.
To listen. To hear.
To smell. To do more than eat.
I would need to taste. To feal;
and feel.

Like with this monkey-fist of an apple.
I would need to bite
the sweet and tart, balanced
like well-wrought justice,
by a blindfolded beauty,
sheet hanging over a wise breast.

I would need to wonder
how this apple came to me.
Did it grow on home base
to children learning fairness
in a game of stickball?
Surely it is not from the apple tree
under which I had my first kiss .
The first time I tasted
the longing to link
to beauty. Apple-wine
too strong for 80lbs of eighth grader.
I became very drunk under that apple tree.
Drunk on Woman. Drunk on curves. Drunk
on borrowed beauty.

Twenty Wild Decembers

Love awoke too soon and I was ready,
too ready,
to become a willing alcoholic.
Many years of haze and hangover followed.

Remembering and munching to the core,
where seeds tinged with cyanide
peak through. Filled with the memory
of the fruit Eve first held. A distant uncle
to this apple I have eaten
to the very core.
Fig-leaved and crouching, fire-hardening
my long spear, carefully buried
between naked ribs, unremembered.

No one has time to notice.
No one has time to wonder.
We eat for energy.
Not to be pressed for a response.
Not to be changed.
Not to be pounded into wisdom
by the hammers of our senses,
by the hammers of our reason,
by the hammers of wonder.

Curiosity killed the cat
and resurrected it a lion.
But no one, these days, has time to roar.

Poems on Time

FIRST KISS

T.S. Eliot was my first kiss.
We stood under the eave just outside my underground
apartment.
My underground apartment on "D" Street
with ceilings too short for my taller friends,
while it rained in rolling torrents.
The sheets and drops slid and gathered
on Spring's greening leaves
to fall onto the root-raised walkway.
of cement wigwams through the grass.
Prufrock's rolled trouser showing ankle
and mermaids singing
into our locked lips.

Suddenly present.
Suddenly aware
that others were here too.
That others were here.
That others were.

Smell of warm rain wetting hot cement.
Cabbie driving by, embarrassed by the PDA,
aware that I am not alone
Suddenly not alone.

There is no second chance for a first kiss.
So special it can only be given once.
And though I know many have had Eliot before me.
For me he will always be
my first kiss.

Twenty Wild Decembers

RESEARCH, NAKED RESEARCH

Does one glimpse of beauty,
pure and naked as a naiad,
ruin, ever-after, every normal cup of tea?
Or does a nymph's golden, laughing sigh
hiding in library aisles
glow warmth into every cold white tile?

What else could keep him,
that white-haired and bent old man,
coming back to the stacks again and again?
Keep him caning his three-legged race with the sand
for one more trip to that land;
for one more touch from the nymph's white hand.

The wink of sly marginalia
only the scholar has known.
The slinking echo of bright bacchanalia
where footnotes have become overgrown.
The nymph's peal echo's off herringbone
in memories of her curving hip,
beating within his breastbone.

Poems on Time

JESUS IS THE BEAUTIFUL GATE
Acts 3

Jesus is the Beautiful Gate
through whom we walk and laugh and leap
into the presence of God the choreographer.

We join the sphere-dance like kings.
Join the sun, leaping and dancing,
covered lightly in light.

As Christ's Life-Word
bubbles and leaps—alive in the dance—
within us. Stopped springs suddenly re-dug.

De-roof my heart.
Let down this paralyzed soul
to wind up a bucket of living water

To pour it out in sermon-song.
To un-dry the desert dust
that this cactus might fruit, might flower.

That it might be poured to fill the trough
of young calves, freed from their stalls
to walk and laugh and leap.

Twenty Wild Decembers

Poems on Time

Saturday

Twenty Wild Decembers

Poems on Time

PEACE WITH THE FALLEN LEAVES

I've made peace with the fallen leaves.
I see in them the fate reserved for me.

Budding green, bursting life,
Lifted down into deep gold-brown.

Glory hoarded into corners.
Mourners massing in pyre-ready piles.

I see heaped there a fate reserved for me,
thus I've made peace with the fallen leaves.

Twenty Wild Decembers

OLD MAN AT THE BLUEBERRY BUSHES

Blueberry bushes
brush bungling hands.
Hands heavy with age
—quivering unhelpfully—
gather taste gushing
gems of tang.
No rot. No root-break.
The ripped branches
are simply savaged off
by shaking old hands.
Hands tired of being bound-
back for decades.
Held mute by manners
monastic and proper.
Held still by habit
and a fury hell hath not.
Hands that now shimmy with the shrubbery
and gambol with the bushes.
Hands that dance harder
the closer to freedom they hover.
But the blueberry bramble
hasn't quite let them be
free as a bobbing bird
lifting broad wings to soar.
Wings steadily slinging
past saturnine light.
Because the bushes still hold
berries worth gathering.
a fortune worth sticking hands
through thorns and thistles for.
Life still holds
treasures that the fallen
—with still and steady hands—
have not the substance to taste.

Poems on Time

WORD-WEAVER

Shuttle runs to meet with the raddle.
Bobbins unspin at the tug of the riddle.
The Weaver of wordings, with finger-flight winding,
levers the weavings of lives in their striving.

For furry-souled flesh still fights with the Spirit.
Christ haunted canticles kill us to kill it.
When lifted within us, we stretch for the finespun
levers of lighting that loom as we live them.

A life that is dead exists in the whispers
of listless and soulless gray ghosty gorillas.
But whispers of death mean that once there was life.
Words that once roared are now murmured and tight.

But those that have ears taste words that are spoken.
Those that have ears smell the verbal that's severed
from life and from light and eternity's even.
Foible-filled jars of clay limping, careening.

Spoken and spoken, the told in the telling,
we die and we live, and we live in the felling.
Held down and out, with plying and sighing.
Until the optics are shown in the dying,

(only the shuttle and winder and bobbin),
as life's actors wag all the way to the coffin.
Autumnal in foibles and wintertide-chested,
the players keep playing their parts unmolested.

The Spring-Weaver sings. The gravedigger quarrys.
The theater of glory is selving through stories.
Upheld by Ghost-writing, through winter's patrolling,
in vernal yarn-spinning the words keep on rolling.

Twenty Wild Decembers

THE ENFEEBLING YEARS

The years that continually enfeeble my body
Are the same years that strengthen my soul.
Though the strength of soul that is gained in these years
is knowledge of how feeble I am alone.

Poems on Time

GOD-HAUNTED GARDEN

The sacred woods have gone rite-silent
not even whispering under their leaves.
I have not the expertise to know
if it is relief or a symptom of grief.

For the pagans all knew that the power was woven
into the branches and into the root.
Pulled from the dirt that was cursed from the first
but jailed by our reaching for wood-given fruit.

This god-haunted garden, once lived in, once loved,
with arched gate of iron, whilom perfectly pearled,
is now rusted and shut, brim-filled with silence,
flawlessly veiled and silent as death.

The profane wood, new-freed to be nature,
shouts now by pointing both inward and up.
Trees throw their heads like a string of wild horses,
fruiting and feeding and lifting their crop.
But dying men, drunk on the Water of Life,
have still more fire than such living ice.

Twenty Wild Decembers

Poems on Time

GLOSSARY

It is probably both pompous and hubristic to put a glossary in the back of my own set of poetry. And yet, here I am, doing it anyway. The reason is simple. I want you reading poetry and not hunting for a dictionary. I never use a word in a poem that I do not believe is exactly the right word to capture my meaning. Communicating what I truly believe; that is my first goal while writing poetry. But having spent my investing years studying theological and philosophical debate, I know that the importance of the right word for accurate communication is paramount. I have no desire to deal in lies. Especially in glorifying lies with meter and verse. True Truth, bursting bonds. That is my desire.

And thus, a glossary. Hopefully it allays confusion and helps you enjoy the poems themselves.

Beggarly Elements - The animistic spirits, imperial genies, and idols of the Old Covenant that held the nations in fear through the misuse of their authority. See Galatians 4:9

Behear - To give your ear to. Listen carefully and intently.

Bulwarked - To have built a defensive wall

Chronos - The Greek god Time, who was a Titan that helped form and create the present world.

Cilia - Microscopic nose hair that move rhythmically to catch and clear dirt and mucus from the airway.

Cockerel - A young domesticated rooster

Twenty Wild Decembers

Crankcase - The housing of the crankshaft in a combustion engine. The crankshaft is what transforms the engines combustion into motion.

Daughters of Ocean - Rivers. According to Hesiod, Ocean marries Tethys and they have three-thousand daughters that become rivers.

Dipteral - The two rows of columns that surround the peristyle Greek Temple

Doggerel - Dog-ugly poetry.

Eli, Eli, lama sabachthani? - My God, my God. Why have you forsaken me? See Mark 15:34.

Enfeeble - Make weak. Dilapidate.

Ephemeral - Transitory, fleeting, or temporary.

Epithet - An adjective or descriptive phrase expressing a quality characteristic. Usually a term of abuse.

Feal - Northern Middle English from Old Norse *fela* - to hide, conceal; cognate with Gothic *filhan* - to hide, bury; Old English feolan - faithful; Old French *feal* and Latin F*idelis* - loyal

Feral - Wild and untamed.

Fettered - Chained up, usually as a slave.

Firebirds - A class of small birds having brilliant orange or red feathers (the tanager, flycatcher, oriole, etc.)

Gambol - To frolic and dance playfully.

Gestation - Womb development.

Poems on Time

Rock of Gibraltar - A giant limestone rock at the end of the Isthmus Peninsula off of Spain. It was one of the Pillars of Hercules that marked the edge of the known and inhabitable world for the Ancient Greeks. Because was a strategic point for both Axis the Allies, it was fought over in World War II.

Goshen - A land in Egypt like the Garden of Eden. Israel settled there and it was protected from the Ten Plagues of Moses - See Genesis 45:10; Exodus 8:22, 9:26

Gristled - Made inedible either because it is cartilage or because it is burned.

Guise - Likeness or appearance. It came into English through an Old French transliteration of the Old German word *Wise*, which means wise.

Idiopath - One of a kind

Iesus Nazarenus, Rex Iudaeorum - Latin for Jesus of Nazareth, King of the Jews. Pontius Pilate had this posted in Greek, Latin, and Hebrew on the cross above Jesus when he was crucified (See Luke 23:38).

Ἰησοῦς ὁ Ναζωραῖος ὁ βασιλεὺς τῶν Ἰουδαίων - Greek for Jesus of Nazareth, King of the Jews. Pontius Pilate had this posted in Greek, Latin, and Hebrew on the cross above Jesus when he was crucified (See Luke 23:38).

Jackboot - A tall military boot used as a symbol of oppression.

Lation - From astronomy or astrology - Motion of a celestial object from one place to another. The movements of heavenly objects relative to one another.

Leaf-mold - Decaying leaves that make for good soil.

Twenty Wild Decembers

Littoral - situated on the shore of a body of water, usually the sea.

Loam - Soil filled with degraded biological material, good for growing things.

Lodestar - A guide star that is used to steer a ship.

Monomaniacal - An inordinate or obsessive zeal for a single idea or thing.

Monopole - A single sided magnetic pole, which is impossible and unnatural.

Muleteer - A driver of tha stubborn old animal the mule.

Mulish - Stubborn like a mule.

Noseblind - Unable to smell.

Pedantry - Excessive attention to detail. From the Greek *Pedegogans*, through the Middle French *Pedante* for teacher.

Petrichor - A pleasant smell that frequently accompanies the first rain after a long period of warm, dry weather.

Petrapentateuch - Stone law of five parts.

Phantasmagoric - A series of ghostly or horrific images.

Polyphemus - The Cyclops that Odysseus blinded. Having only one eye, the Cyclopes had no depth perception. They lived without a city and without political organization, and therefore were unable to form community. So they also had no access to the perception of others.

Psalter - The Psalms of David arranged for singing.

Poems on Time

Pyre - A place to burn the dead

Raca - Aramaic term for expressing anger with someone. See Matthew 5:22.

Riposte - A quick unplanned responsive retaliation in fencing. A quick and unthoughtful jibe in conversation.

Saturnine - Gloomy, slow, having to do with the planet Saturn, or the Greek God Chronos.

Sepulcher - A crypt or cave-tomb

String of horses - Horses kept by a single person or family or horses tied together for a particular task or trip.

Vestral - The vestry is the room where pastor's put on their vestments in order to lead a congregation in the liturgy of a church service.

Vibrissae - Nose hair. From the Latin Vibrāra, meaning to vibrate or to sway.

Whelmed - Engulfed , submerged, or buried.

Whet - To sharpen a sword, knife, or ax.

Whilom - Anglo-Saxon for formerly or in the past.

Wyrm - Anglo Saxon for dragon or large serpent.

Yeshua Ha'Netzeret V'mlech Ha'Yehudim - Hebrew for Jesus of Nazareth, King of the Jews. Pontius Pilate had this posted in Greek, Latin, and Hebrew on the cross above Jesus when he was crucified (See Luke 23:38).

ABOUT THE AUTHOR

Jason Farley is a Classical Literature teacher at The Oaks Academy in Spokane, WA. He attended Greyfriars Pastors Hall and was ordained as a Christian minister in 2008. He blogs at The Westminster Confession of Funk (crosspolitic.com/jasonfarley). He is also the general editor of Jovial Press (jovial-pub.com) and loves helping writers, especially poets, make it to publication.

Jason is around the social medias @jasonfarleys and he loves to hear from readers. You can email him direct at happyfattitude@gmx.com.

You can find more books from Jovial Press and sign up for our main list at www.jovial-pub.com.

Make sure to check out Jason's children's book
<u>Waiting through Winter,</u>
illustrated by Jessica Linn Evans,
available wherever you buy your books.

Time ends in a garden too.

www.ingramcontent.com/pod-product-compliance
Lightning Source LLC
Chambersburg PA
CBHW031456040426
42444CB00007B/1126